DISSONANCE

NAVIGATING THROUGH THE ENTWINED HEARTS OF MALE-FEMALE DYNAMICS

PUNISWARY P.

Made with ♥ on the Notion Press Platform
www.notionpress.com

Dedicated to every man and woman who believes that when it comes to love relationships or marriage, they are making better and wiser decisions than their parents!

Contents

FOREWORD

This book may be useful in shedding light on some of the attitudes and behaviors of men and women in love relationships or marriage life today, which may prompt readers to examine their own relationships and make better efforts to keep their partnerships going.

PREFACE

Dissonance is a book that discusses the disagreements that frequently arise in romantic relationships between men and women. What causes it to happen initially? Is it only because of the circumstances that stand in their way, or is it because of their own high standards, attitudes, and demanding actions?

By reading this book, you can gain even more insights from the author's perspective.

Acknowledgements

Indebted to God!
Obligated to my Family!
Thankful to my Human Diary!
Last but not the least...
Appreciative to all my Friends and Well Wishers!

Prologue

This book is divided into a few parts that discuss the rationale of today's men and women, which is not very acceptable, particularly in romantic relationships. They believe that pushing for what they deserve or asking more of their relationship is the best way to keep it going, something their parents failed to do earlier. As a result, they believe that their way of life is far wiser and better than their parents.

They have no idea that their twisted perspective will not serve them well or for very long. Even if they are able to take their relationship to the next level and get married, they will still experience a lot of dissonance between them most of the time, which could make them wonder what went wrong in the first place. However, until they alter the way they understand and perceive key factors, they will not receive the solution.

Agreeable that it is everyone's rights to their own thought process and how to carry on with their relationship, but at the same time, I do feel that, as a writer, it is also my freedom to put my ideas into words in order to enlighten those who are willing to learn more about their uniqueness. I hope that this book will at least illuminate one person, at the very least, to view some aspects in a clearer, easier-to-understand manner rather than confounding them.

I

Aversion of Being Binded

A committed romantic relationship requires two people who are ready to give it their all. Most significantly, for the relationship to be well-protected, a great deal of resilience as well as sturbonness are required in holding onto it, staying with the partner through thick and thin, and fighting for what is right. Even if these sound fierce and difficult, but love is simple and straightforward. Anyone who truly loves their partner will not find this difficult to do, since they will naturally provide their partner all of these things without being asked. If you find it difficult to consider all these in a relationship, consider again whether you truly love the other person.

Some would object to these kinds of interpretations. To demonstrate that they are not thinking the same as their parents, the majority of men and women today like introducing weird ideas. They claim that their parents have only made poor decisions and have not been strong enough to stand for themselves to part ways when it does not benefit them greatly. Staying together with each other in spite of every lows in life simply indicates that they have been dumb or unhappy all along. Today's couples are adept at breaking up with each other when things get difficult in order to prevent making blunders like these. They believe it is the correct thing to do since they want to live a happy and peaceful life.

However, isn't it more satisfying to feel all kind of positive and negative emotions towards a single individual for many years rather than experiencing them again with many different people in shorter duration?

No, most of the couples today will not be able to foresee any kind of satisfaction from this theory.

They would like to claim that they will leave relationships when they are unable to tolerate anything that goes against their souls because they have a clearer mind and will not "settle for less" since they feel that they deserve better. Though you have made decisions that are likely better than those of your parents, there are some things you will never be able to accomplish in their shoes. These include learning to be content with what you have, sticking with someone through good times and bad, and fighting to rebuild the connection. Since they should be a partner who can only experience the nice and positive aspects of someone, they believe that fighting for what is rightfully theirs is obviously "toxic" and that it is not their responsibility to support someone through their low points. If you try to be anything other than that, it simply indicates that you are settling for less.

Generally, they do not consider it fortunate to be with someone who is still affected by past trauma or who is not fully recovered. They consider it to be in a terrible relationship. The world of today will teach you that you should not be with them, support their healing, or assure them that you will not subject them to any further trauma. Having to demonstrate to them that you would stay with the person regardless will be seen as you are being sinful to yourself because it is a huge work to be done which should have been done by the individual and his or her family but not you because you deserve better - someone who treats you like a king or queen and offers you a sweet relationship with a lot of benefits! You will want them to comprehend your trauma and respond to it appropriately, yet you shouldn't be there to aid in their recovery.

Although you see the world so much better than your parents did, you should not expect to be able to keep any of the relationships longer like your parents had since your view of modern life is never going to line up with anything that would last. You will never be content with anything that comes your way if you don't stop searching. You'll keep looking for more beneficial things from more individuals, but you won't be able to find the one you're looking for since your search will never come to an end and you'll never be satisfied with anyone that you meet. "He or she is enough for me; I will accept them for who they are" - is not a definition found in today's dictionary. They will always desire someone who is always improving themselves—not for the benefit of the other person, but rather for their own advantages.

People today try to shy away from commitments in order to prevent situations like these. Because if they are in committed partnerships, they believe that they will be required to handle a lot of responsibilities. They tend to invent a lot of intriguing but confusing terms, like "situationship," "friends with benefits," "besties," "getting to know" phase, "seeing or talking to someone" phase, "someone whom I potentially can be in relationship with" phase, "dating many" at the same time, and so on, in order to enjoy the benefits of being in a relationship even before they are in one. These words are obviously intended to serve the one and only function which is allowing any side to end the relationship at any time with no difficulty on their behalf.

They would naturally experience some sort of dissonance between them because their expectations for the partnership are different if one of them feels the need to be there for each other simply because they have traveled together almost as a couple and what is a bigger deal just to get into relationship and lead the path to marriage. "Just because I've done this or we've behaved almost like a couple, that doesn't mean I should get into a relationship with them," "Just because I'm in relationship with this person, that doesn't mean I should get married to him or her" - are how lots of people think about it these days. Nowadays, nobody dates with the intention of getting married. To them, marriage is a completely different chapter, with a lot of conditions and standards to be fulfilled before they could call themselves husbands or wives.

Even if they believe they are making better decisions than their parents, they are self-assured enough and do not see it as humorous or embarrassing to say that their parents have had more complicated lives than they have.

II

"Love Spell" on Men

The majority of women nowadays who assert that they are more independent, strong, intelligent, and well-educated also have a distinct mindset and believe that they have achieved greater success than others. However, women are primarily designed to be glorified by masculinity. To be put in another way, most people assume that men should be able to live up to the expectations of women when it comes to love relationship. These kinds of women are smart enough to choose the kind of men that they can live with. They only pick and target the genuine and loyal ones, not the difficult and complicated ones.

Even if the woman is independent, she still has needs to be well taken care of, and a man should be able to support both himself and her on a constant basis. If men are not financially strong, this may purposefully set off a chain reaction that causes them to feel insecure or inferior, but that is not the aim being addressed. The significant aspect of this is that men need to be able to provide and should do so even if it means using up all of their power or energy. This is due to the fact that they have an obligation to make sure that their women feel fully safe, comfortable, and well-protected in this relationship. The woman may not be asking for his money directly because she must already be making money, but what she really wants is to see what type of efforts he can do to overwhelm her with their connection.

She doesn't seem to be interested in your money, but rather support her by providing her with ostentatious goods like jewelry, gadgets, or accessories in the hopes of living up to her expectations. If you wanted to live up to her expectations and make her happy, you would have to do it. All she wanted was for her standards and expectations to be met, particularly "if you are not up to her mark." Do not confuse that it is because she is interested in your money because it is a whole separate chapter. If you truly want to get married and spend the rest of your life with her, instead make a significant financial, emotional, and effort investment to achieve this.

He wouldn't have the clarity to even start any of these to live up to her expectations if he was a tough or complicated man that was involved with her. Now, do you understand why these women do not target these kinds of men?

In addition, a number of factors need to be taken into account to determine whether a woman is content in her relationship. Many women view little things as not so little. The petty little things that a man ought to do while spending time with her which women nowadays call it as "bare minimum" like continue showing affection, love and care multiple times even if she is difficult. On the other hand, he must be offering to pay her first during most of their datings. He is a total failure if he is unable to accomplish that. In fact, if she is spending more money than him on their outing together, naturally it's a pride for her. "I paid for it, I did not make him to pay for us" - she likes to mention it countless times just to prove indirectly that she is not interested in his money.

Not to mention the extra-fitting actions like pulling out their chair at the table so she can be comfortably seated first, opening the car doors for her to sit in the car respectfully, letting her enter the building by opening the door of the space they are in, making sure she is properly protected while she is feeling ill, to honor her with gifts and much more in return. Prior to your presence in her life, she would have lived on her own terms and taken care of herself independently in the entire time. However, once you choose her and want her in your life, you must always go above and beyond to prevent her from coming to believe that having you in her life is not worth it. In the end, she may not do the same for you in return by giving your needs and wish lists enough importance but that is not crucial because ultimately, she will be needed to prioritized in order to be kept and for you to sustain the relationship. In fact, she would be anticipating some interesting praises for her efforts if she had offered you some support or helped you in any way to grow as a person. Why is it necessary to identify her contribution or require recognition if she did it with sincerity? Alternatively, might it be argued that she didn't support you, but rather did it out of pride?

Apart from it, wait as much as you can wait and do it even if you can't do it more! It is only a reflection of your desire and effort to spend time with her that you should wait for minutes, hours, or even longer to be able to see her in a day. A few years later, these gestures might change, but women would still be curious to know how much that they are respected. Nevertheless, you should never force a woman to wait for you, even for a single second, as this will only come across as condescending. Men should be able to prioritize their relationships with friends and family at the same time. If she agrees, then you can concentrate on your buddies or spend more time with them. If not, you must cease your current activity to augment her sense of fulfillment in this relationship. She may additionally ask you to value her over your friends. Placing her on the same level as your pals could be the least expected.

So, what is so bad in doing this?

Ultimately, everything revolves around putting her first. But, how can a man put his life partner, friends, and family at the same priority level? You absolutely can. It's not as hard as it sounds since you can multitask and fulfill everyone's expectations, even if it means pretending to be someone you're not or failing at other aspects in life. Even though you are a family-oriented man and put your parents or siblings first, you should not listen to them because you should already know what you want out of life. It will be perceived that you are not listening to your own intuition and that you are demeaning your partner if you obey your family. You could have followed your family's instruction throughout your life since birth, but the moment you pick her as your partner in your life, you have to stop what you were doing before her presence in life; no matter how important is that for you. Even if you reply, "No, this is what I wanted to do; this is not what my family says." But if this is not what she desires in a relationship, you would still be perceived as showing her contempt. In the end, you'll be forced to the verge of collapse in some way.

However, it would sound unjust or impolite to her if you pester her to manage her love, friendships and family at the same time. It could appear as though you are disobeying her or that you are expecting her to alter her way of life to suit your needs. They may even go for some me-time for themselves with lesser distraction even if it means going for a break with no contact or ghosting their man but you should always stay in the closest possible touch. Her ability to be herself would be in disarray if you are not allowing her to have some alone time. In case you try to tell your partner that you need some "Me-Time," she might try to question you, "What's up?" "What's not right? You need Me-Time—but why? What's the deal? Is that anything that we need to discuss? Speak with me. Why aren't you sharing something with me?" This could even result in fights and prevent you from having any alone time. They would try to convince you that they are there for you in your hours of need, but you wouldn't realize that you are a person with a life of your own and that you should have some alone time. Despite this, you would end up forfeiting your personal time for the duration of the relationship or marriage. On clearer note, indeed, you would lose some space to breath for yourself.

"Love Spell" on Men by their Woman! Men would not understand that they are in a bittersweet spell's dillema in the name of love and they would naturally believe that this is how they should be in love relationship as per their woman's expectations.

In order to fight and make this point, women would argue that a relationship is about two people. "If you are unable to spend time with your partner, be a good companion, or communicate everything together, then stay out of it!", they will insist.

Yes, they are correct, but they would also argue against it by saying things like, "Let her live her life; don't make her change it for you just because you're in a relationship with her."

Men should keep working to make women feel like they are a part of a team, but women should have their own time and lives.

III
Women's Magic Trick

Gentlemen, you deserve this, so handle it. You chose her based on your ludicrous facts, so deal with it. What drew you to her could have been anything—her appearance as she could have been the most attractive woman in the group, her career, her fun and playful side, her independence and childishness—or any combination of these factors. However, it wouldn't have been based on her true character or personality (apart from the false or fake persona she initially adopts), as you wouldn't have picked these women as your partners in the first place if that were the case.

That being said, the best part is that even after you have done all for your partner, you might still see her turning away from the relationship. It might be the case that you were unable to adjust or transform yourself in response to one or any of the issues she highlighted. You have to realize that following them all without ignoring minor factors too, is what improves you as a person, in her opinion. It doesn't matter how much of yourself you put into the relationship. It doesn't matter how hard you work to keep this relationship going or repair it. It doesn't matter how far you can take this relationship or yourself. Your ability to comply, obey, and adjust to her expectations is what matters most of this relationship, as those are the only lists that would be useful to you personally.

DISSONANCE!

Even though you might be skilled in another area, failing to adapt to what she exactly wants could still put you in danger since she would still say, "I want someone who can do this." She will add up by saying, "Try to fix this; it will help you to be a better person in the future." Both of you will be in a conflict on whose way to follow but you would automatically think that this is the nature of love and that she is doing you a favor by improving you. "She is so kind. She is attempting to assist me in becoming a better person. She won't ever harbor something bad for me. She must be correct," your instant thought tells you, and you will choose to follow it. This will help her to commit to the relationship better and longer as you fulfilling what she wants and this will make her happier to stay. The most important thing in this situation is that your woman is happy in their own unique interpretation of balanced relationships, even though the entire journey may cause you to lose yourself.

Men tend to focus most of their attention on their work, passion, or other external matters; their partner may not comprehend what's going on, but if their expectations aren't met, it will lead to disputes. Men would automatically solve half of the trivial issues if they were to realize that they fall short of their partners' expectations. Men would expect their partner to allow them some time and not apply more pressure at that point, but it's more of a question of how many women are able to do that. Because their expectations will keep getting in the way and forcing them to keep looking for it, and the guys will eventually feel compelled to do it anyhow, if only to get the job done and stay out of trouble. And why the man is not content or happy with what they are doing for their woman would then be a question that women would ask their partners. If the man is not happy that he could meet her expectations? Another problem would arise, and so, the man would choose to act as though he is the most content to meet her needs in order to avoid having to explain it.

Using the well-known Indian film industry pair as an example, millions of people would find admiration for them. Not mentioning their names but they look great together and are really fortunate to be regarded as one of the most attractive couples in the industry. But in the majority of her interviews, she would say things like, "He's a fantastic father and a wonderful husband," about her partner. He takes care of the kids in every manner possible, even monitoring their schedules when I'm away on the shoot. He makes sure that I have no limitations and that I can pursue my work and personal goals. Additionally, he makes sure that no one at home says anything bad about me. I haven't prepared anything substantial as in normal cooking for him in exchange. He does, however, pretty much everything for me. He is like my Godfather".

A fascinating couple, but the key to their success is that she finds happiness in him, and his attempts to elevate and glorify her are what have allowed her to stay and maintain their relationship for so long, almost 18 years of marriage life —unfortunately, not many people are aware of this. They love this pair unquestioningly. When asked how they choose the movies for their careers during a different interview, she responded right away, saying, "My projects are my projects; he doesn't say much about it, but his projects are mine. I'm aware that he chooses interesting stories, but we still need to talk about it." The host smiled at the humor that was made there, but it was not evident what sort of power she had as his wife to talk about his career—but, he didn't have the same when it came to her ideas. Under the video, the most common comment was, "What kind of amazing couple they are." "They just love each other, how I wish to have a husband like him." "They are the best couple that I've seen, they just understand each other so much, not many can be like this." "They are so inspiring."

On stage, the actor once beamingly said, "I'm thankful to my wife for allowing me to continue to act in movies." Such a powerful statement from him demonstrates how much he values her in his life, but little did he realize that she was advancing in her career with a number of intriguing films, all the while claiming that her husband is the cornerstone of it, granting her every wish in her career and allowing her to pursue her passions but when it is for him, she grants him "permission" to continue acting.

Folks, take a lengthy exhalation and welcome to reality! Does any woman who reads this feel angry or frustrated for bringing something up that is pertinent to men's wellbeing? Ladies, try posing a question to yourself. If you are in a relationship—whether it is fresh or has been a long time—why are you still in it? What keeps you in this relationship? What was it that you saw or got from this relationship that helped you continue on this path? You may also try asking the same questions to your girlfriend, wife or any other woman in a relationship if you're a man seeking to acquire more from this.

The majority of their answers would be, "He is so affectionate. He is a nice person, and he makes sure that my needs are fulfilled. He will not take me for granted. He would chase after me all the time if I was upset with him, and the more I ignore him, the more fun this relationship would be. I could hang up on him, and he would call me back. He is making sure that I'm worthy. He constantly makes efforts to see me smiling and happy. He is making me feel so comfortable that I can be myself with him. He respects me and does every little thing for me to be content. He loves and protects me all the time. He would go all the way out of his comfort zone just to spend time with me, he will still put continuous effort to be with me even if I am pushing him away, he gave me the confidence for me to return back to him whenever I want to and that he will accept me immediately and so on."

There could be more reasons, but mostly the reasons would be how much she is acknowledged and appreciated on this journey. It would be extremely rare for a woman to say these kind of simple sentences like, "I'm in this relationship with him because he deserves good and great things in life. I'm trying my best to keep him loved and feeling worthy. His journey is tough and I choose to stay in this relationship just so he know that I am behind his back to support him during his downfall. He will just need to be treated right, and I'm here for that, and that is why I'll sustain this relationship."

Women would become agitated the moment they read this and respond, "Well, there should be two ways! How could it be one way only? The man needs to think the same as well".

You are correct, my darling lady.

"Two ways relationship" is coming to the picture only when you are at the point to think if you are contributing to his betterment and peace or not.

Didn't it strike it to you while you are accepting all his extra efforts to fulfill your expectations?

There must be mutual reciprocation and two ways but this only becomes apparent to you when you find yourself in a position where you are questioned if you make him feel worthy, content, and happy without expecting anything in return. NOTIONAL and UNCONDITIONAL ones. It is unusual that you consider what you can offer without conditions while you are at the receiving end, absorbing all of his extra effort on your behalf. According to you, giving him presents on his birthdays and constantly speaking with him over the phone or via video calls while exchanging fascinating tales about the whole day, texting, laughing, arguing, cajoling each other and being prioritized perhaps a bit less than his parents but siblings and friends should be after you as well as to get your needs and requests being fulfilled by him—is what love and being in a relationship are all about.

Denying this, perhaps?

IV

Men are Indecisive

Why are men constantly expected to treat women according to a predetermined set of criteria, while women are not treating the men in the same way? Excerpts about how men ought to be treated are scarce. A quote from a random source stated that "Men deserve to be gifted too" makes it sound so unjust to think that gifts are only for women. There was another quote that said, "You'll be surprised at how many issues in your relationship will disappear if you show her that she is your priority and remember to show her how much you care." Whoa, what a lovely quote that perfectly captures what's expected today. To avoid troubles in a relationship, all women need to accomplish is to be prioritized, be reminded of how much their men care about them, and what sort of efforts that men are making to handle everything with ease. Done! This makes both of you pleased.

Refusing to accept this still?

Nonetheless, for few women, appearance and face beauty may not come naturally to them, but inner beauty is boundless. There exist females who embody the exact opposite of the aforementioned characteristics. Instead of having a lot of demands or expectations, they are more of an unconditional giver. With no requirements at all, occasionally. They only desired for him to be happy and to have everything he is entitled to. All they wanted was for him to receive everything he is due and to be treated fairly and highly respected. The real, authentic ones, where the man may feel more at ease to talk, learn, and strive towards improving themselves on their own pace without fear of being left by their woman. They do exist, yes. Although these women should be treasured forever, a new issue will arise.

With these kinds of women, what do men do?

Being around these women lacks flavor since there aren't enough hurdles for males to overcome. Men love to chase after women; if they are obtaining everything they need from them effortlessly, they are not interested in pursuing them.

Oh, that's wonderful! You bemoan the fact that women are difficult to manage, claiming that they are complex and that it is impossible to satisfy their demands and wants while you brush off a woman who readily offers everything to you without asking for much in return. You are aware that she would stop at nothing to maintain your happiness and sense of worth. She would exert every effort possible. She would go above and beyond to support and assist you in whatever way you needed, but you would only take her for granted, treat her as if she had been unimportant, or even keep her as a last resort so you could take your time reciprocating because you knew that no matter what, she would always be there for you.

You might not look good either, but since looks have become your top priority, you would expect the most attractive girl to be your partner. If she proves to be tough to handle but has the same great appearance as you wanted, you still whine about how difficult women are. You feel that she is being overly needy, clingy, and inconsiderate when she tries too hard to be with you, and you get upset when she doesn't try at all and expects you to try hard for her, too, since you have to give it your all and nothing comes back.

What exactly do you want?

Can we see who is complex and complicated? Men tend to lack clarity about their true desires in life, as evidenced by their willingness to turn down simple solutions to problems they may encounter and instead employ flimsy justifications when faced with them. They would then grumble about how hard and unchanging their lives was.

Dear Genuine and Nice Men, if you have a sincere woman in your life who would give anything that you need with no second thoughts and would never give up on you, even if you put her through tough hurdles, yet you declined her because you were not interested in her since there was no chase or challenge, then question yourself again about what are you doing with your life. You tend to reject this because it is not interesting or satisfactory for you or people around you today, but this is something with a very low level of complexity that would last the longest time because she would not think about her own needs alone but also about you and would not expect a lot from you in the long run. She knows what she wants. She will be herself while giving you the space to be yourself. She knows how to value you, and naturally, if you start to appreciate, respect and acknowledge someone like her in the relationship, then there are only gains that you would be receiving at both ends. This is the utmost priority to make both of you win in a relationship until the end, regardless if it is a love relationship or a married one.

V

Boastful Vanity of Men

Be that as it may, let's potray about some men today who are lack of genuinity and gentleness that chose to behave unfairly with their women that has inner beauty as described earlier. Ordinarily, these kind of men prefer to be in charge of the people they are in relationship with the most. They would still place their partner under them because they consciously think that their physical prowess makes them superior to women. They are adept at controlling their partner without saying it aloud. Some women have chosen to remain with them despite the fact that it would not bring them happiness. They opt to live with this kind of life, even if it might not be worth it to entirely lose their peace and joy for such an inconsiderate man. The majority of the women that cling to these men are gentle and accepting, which makes life simple for the men.

The strong sense of masculinity within the men tend to envision that they can attack their partner easily especially by gaslighting them as the women are on the wrong side all the time along the road. Women with gentle dispositions tend to feel inherently inadequate for their partners, which motivates them to keep working hard to meet their men's demands. Since the men play a psychological game, they will always win as their women will take care of everything without being asked. In the end, what's most astonishing is that these men would never feel bad about what they've done to their partner because, at the end of the day, all they really need is someone who can give them everything they want and treat them like royalty, which proves that they're already on the right track. They are known as narcissists.

Men like them are the sole reason why relationships that can last up to 10- or fifteen-years end in disaster. Even if they won't acknowledge it, they force their women to behave nearly like slaves. These men frequently acquire a great deal of confidence in their ability to manage a relationship in accordance with their lifestyle preferences without needing to be aware of what their partners want. In addition, in a married life, if he is the primary breadwinner for the family, he may decide to maintain complete control over both of their lives in order to support his wife and family. Naturally, his partner would feel more reliant on him, which makes him pleased from within. The fact that he is able to maintain control over her life feels like a tremendous accomplishment.

What if their women are not as portrayed above?

What happens if their ladies are making the same amount of money as the men?

What if the woman are aware of the kind of man they are with and are unwilling to comply with his requests?

Consequently, it wouldn't take long for both of them to start arguing and quarrelling with one another. In the name of defending their relationships for better peace, they would both be eager to share their points of view with one another, but in this process, they would both wind up losing themselves. And, rather than taking responsibility for one's own mistakes, a great deal of blame will be placed on one another.

On a different subject, men are needed to be able to comprehend that a woman does not intend to start a fight when she approaches him to explain the nature of their disagreement or discuss any other aspect of their relationship in a non-confrontational manner; rather, it is her attempt to mend the relationship and do everything within her power to keep it intact. As long as she is making an effort to address the difficulties, it simply demonstrates her concern and her desire for something to improve since she doesn't want things to go worse. But as soon as a woman begins to voice her opinion, the majority of men go into defensive mode, begin defending themselves, attempt to be extremely cruel and mean to her, and cut her off in an effort to get her to say what has to be said.

One of the main reasons on why men need to dispute and register their differences when their women bring up any issues is that these men like to be in charge of others but become quite nervous and insecure when someone else takes over. Their inability to acknowledge that their partners are brighter and smarter than they are will cause them to believe that living with these women will lower their self-esteem. However, rather than owning up to their erroneous, they would prefer to spin and manipulate the whole thing as the fault of the other side. This will become a complete ego clash between both of them.

DISSONANCE!

Furthermore, if they choose to remain together in spite of this, saying that relationships will always have problems and that what matters is how they fight and stick together, this will eventually become a loyalty issue. A man who is generally skilled at boasting and being conceited will simply require someone to serve him without any complaints. He would not think twice and would be extremely vulnerable to look for someone else who could fulfill that if he couldn't obtain it from his girlfriend. The problem of allegiance now arises. He would be more than prepared to deceive his present partner without feeling guilty. They would go so far as to argue that they are acting in this way because their partner is unfit or inappropriate. At the very least, the men would physically abuse their partner in order for her to align with his thoughts and expectations. In addition, he would find joy in it and carry on doing it repeatedly without giving it any consideration if he could observe some favorable improvements in their spouse following the abusive manner.

VI

Influenced by the Globe

Observing numerous happy couples on social media merely serves to reinforce the notion that a pair should only be content and happy. They believe that disagreements, dissonance, and fights are only for the losers. Some well-known influencers who choose to motivate the globe through their inspirational quotes or everyday lives, particularly when it comes to relationships, often present couples as having to follow all the established rules. "Let's be like them," "We have to follow their way to be happy," and "Let's show the world that we are very excited about each other" will be the mindset of some couples as audiences. Their uniqueness or unique ways of expressing their affection for one another will gradually disappear. Couples nowadays have a mindset like this; that no one can stop because social media is everywhere and only shows the positive aspects of life. Influencers on social media, therefore, have a big say in what they post. Sometimes they can reveal more about themselves than just the ideal partner—like sharing their imperfections and growing as a team by accepting one another as well.

For instance, a couple of influencers - Sam and Monica Patterson, coined the term "simulation husband" in their social media videos. It's just another way of stating that her husband always knows the appropriate response to any strange inquiry she has and goes above and beyond to make her happy on a regular basis. It's a depiction of all his kind actions and how much he exalts his wife, never doing anything improper. He is referred to as the "simulation husband" when his contribution to their union is nearly flawless. Yes, such videos are amazing because they demonstrate how sweet a relationship can grow, but the majority of comments by many women on the videos ask questions like, "Can we share your husband?" "If my husband doesn't do this, I don't want him." "How is he so flawless?" "Why does my husband not like him?" and further comments along these lines. These days, people frequently compare things after seeing quick posts like these.

Naturally, Sam and Monica would experience difficult moments together as well, but they showcase their loving, caring side on social media, and viewers often believe what they see. They would start disliking their men because they are not like Sam and would immediately want their mate to be just like him. Although the comments make it seem simple, the effect it has on the audience depends on their daily lives at home. Their videos demonstrate the happiness that the couple could have if they only had to keep elevating and glorifying the woman. Maintaining a pleasant relationship with your partner is all about saying and doing kind things to her. Once more, the focus is on your woman's contentment and serenity, and maintaining the connection will be simpler for you, as mentioned earlier.

Another example of a social media influencer is a man who would share amazing quotes that most audiences could connect to, preaching about life and relationships. Not revealing the influencer's name, but if you know, you know. He wrote books on how to alter our perceptions better and even offered audio advice like podcasts on how to handle our partners in relationships, particularly on understanding their manipulation and toxicity and deciding whether to stay or leave. Some quotes that he supports and shares on his page go like this:

"Be careful. Manipulation can feel like love."

"My mom said, "Waiting for someone to act correctly is a disrespect to yourself. You're compromising your worth just because someone can't fully afford it."

"When people fall in love with someone's flowers, but not their roots, they don't know what to do when autumn comes. Your relationships need to be built on deep alignment on values, character and morals (the roots), not just "love" appearance, hobbies and status (the flowers)."

Wonderful statements, however, they do not line up with his wife's video, which shows how untidy he can be as a husband. He essentially left everything partly done and disorganized at home, leaving the wife to tidy up and maintain order. Every husband is the same, according to what she posted. It's odd, though, because while he is blogging about how someone shouldn't wait for someone else to act appropriately in a relationship because that's disrespectful and they shouldn't settle with that behavior, his wife is actually expecting him to perform appropriately as her spouse as well. Isn't that inconsiderate to his spouse? Or will he assert that all husbands act in the same manner and they are just minor factor?

In addition, he shared a different video in which he responds with a constant "Wow" whenever his wife enthusiastically tells the same story like the first time. Yes, the video may have been posted in jest, but isn't that also in opposition to his previous statement that manipulation can feel like love? Will he claim that listening to her excitedly on her repeating the same narrative is just out of respect and not manipulation? Is it a sincere admiration for his wife in the first place?

On the other hand, The Ace Family is made up of Christine and Austin McBroom, well-known social media influencers who share videos of their everyday activities, challenges, and pranks. Recently, there was a widely shared story about how the couple's impending divorce has destroyed the family. Furthermore, there are many accusations against the husband that he cheated on her with another woman. The reality is still unknown, even though Austin has refused these kinds of claims. However, many people are still believing that he would be the only reason that this entire family is breaking. His wife said in a social media post that their paths as a couple had changed and that, this has led to unreconcilable challenges. "I have spent the past few years honoring my commitment to my family and putting my children first; all the while, I seemed to be losing myself and my own personal happiness," she continued. But Austin has stated publicly that getting a divorce is the hardest thing he has ever had to decide.

There could be any number of reasons why this is breaking down. What's really absurd is that the same people who are criticizing him and stressing how important honesty and loyalty are in a relationship are also the ones who were hoping to meet a man like Austin earlier. Perhaps, the audience is right that he has cheated on her, or perhaps there's another reason. However, initially their videos with a lot of love and a cute, romantic vibe have consistently garnered millions of views. For instance, a video of Austin staring at his wife while she was engaged in another activity went viral. The same video was shared by viewers with different captions, like "Get you a man who stares at you like this." "The kind of man that I want." "The man who would stare at you like this will be the genuine one." and so on. The funniest part of the video was the comments that followed, where the majority of women would say that they wish they could date someone like Austin. "If my man doesn't stare at me like this, then I don't want him." "I wish I get someone like Austin." "I'm hoping that my man can be like Austin sometimes." and etc.

Additionally, the same video went viral with a different caption after this divorce revelation was made public, saying something like, "He can cheat even if he stares at you like this." Since love, honesty, and loyalty are so important, everyone in the comment section cursed and swore at him. They also felt horrible for Christine and their three children for having to go through this. But what about the kind of comments before this announcement which indicated that they don't want their man if he isn't staring at his partner lovingly like Austin? How come all of these now has taken a backseat while honesty and loyalty are given as the top priorities? Women would want it only when a man is on the verge of betraying them and being disloyal; otherwise, they would be living in a fantasy world where they would demand all that they see on social media. A woman's expectations of her partner are growing increasingly bizarre, particularly in light of the vlogs and videos that social media celebrities post.

Another new trend that has gained traction is the posting of videos showing grooms crying as they watch their wives walk down the aisle to start the wedding ceremony. The majority of women who leave comments on these types of videos seem to think highly of this gesture and even express opinions along the lines like "I don't want him if he doesn't cry like this on my wedding day." "Be right back, let me tell my man to cry like this while I'm walking towards him on the wedding day." "Why didn't my man cry like this on our wedding day?" and so on.

Speaking about social media influencers and disclosing audience comments are entirely up to them; it's possible that they meant them from their heart or that they were making a joke. This particular topic is simply about their cognitive processes; it has nothing to do with restricting someone from doing things they like or from having certain desires in their marriages or relationships.

For these women, let's put it this way: on your wedding day, let your man cry as he watches you approach him down the aisle; let him see you as the greatest blessing and be moved by your approach. While you're concentrating on something else, let him gaze at you as though he's the luckiest man alive, let him exalt and glorify you with numerous perspectives, let him go above and beyond by buying you flowers, chocolates, expensive materials or any other extra gestures that is considered as the modern woman's bare minimum, and then let him betray you by flirting with other women or ending up with someone else.

Can you really accept it?
Why not? How come you can't take it when he cheats since he has put in all the dream contributions that you needed? Is it the case that these actions are all come in a package with loyalty as well? And wouldn't it be more than enough

for you at that point of time if he was being faithful? So why, right from the start, weren't these sufficient for you? For what reason are other strange demands given more priority?

Treat him equitably. Understand the distinctions between your needs and wants in this relationship. Treat him like a king even if he is not making any extra attempts but is being incredibly honest and loyal above what is anticipated. Because he merits and deserves proper treatment.

Otherwise, he needs someone else as his partner in his life to treat him better than you.

The same goes for her too. Her man ought to treat her like a queen as well. Don't write off a kind and true woman who dedicates her entire life to you and your betterment in life whilst acting as though all women are challenging to deal with.

Epilogue

Please refrain from criticizing the author by saying that she is ignorant of the modern world or that her idiosyncratic old-fashioned ideas are foolish. Dissonance has succeeded as intended if even one reader—a man or a woman—who is able to understand the contents written and start to examine their own mental processes, their expectations for their relationship, or even attempts to improve things by changing their perspective.